Budding Biologist

Where Do I Live?

by

Kristine Duehl

illustrated by

Katy Castronovo

Printed and bound in the United States by Self Publishing, Inc.

ISBN 978-0-9855481-1-7

To our husbands, who have always supported our eccentric ambitions.

We would also like to thank all the people who have supported Budding Biologist's expansion, especially Cheryl Coffman and Scott Schmit, whose support helped make this book happen.

Where do you live? Is it cold or hot? Does it rain a lot, or very little? Are there lots of trees or tall grasses?

Biomes are places where plants and animals that need the same kind of rainfall and temperature live together.

For example, some kinds of plants and animals need a hot and dry biome, but different ones live where it is often cool and wet.

There are five basic biomes: tundra, grassland, forest, desert and water.

What kind of biome do you live in?

Let's turn the page to find out more about the biomes.

Tundra

Grassland

Forest

Desert

Water

Where does a fennec fox live?

The fennec fox lives in a hot desert. Deserts get very little rainfall and therefore have few plants.

The fennec fox is nocturnal, meaning it is active at night, because it is cooler at night in the desert. It also has a small body and big ears, which help keep it cool.

What else could you do well if you had big ears?

Where does a cheetah live?

Cheetahs live in hot grasslands, but other kinds of grasslands are cold. Grasslands have tall grasses and a few bushes and trees. They get very little rain, but are not as dry as deserts.

Cheetahs can run really fast, but get tired after about a minute, so they hide in the grass while they rest. The cheetah's spots help it hide when it is sitting in the tall grasses.

What else about the cheetah might help it hide in the yellow grass?

Where does an arctic hare live?

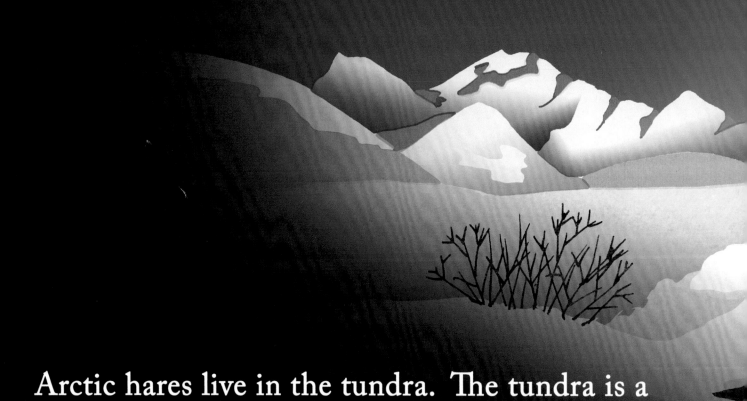

Arctic hares live in the tundra. The tundra is a
windy biome that is dry, cold and icy for most of
the year. Because the tundra is cold and dry, only
short plants are able to survive.

Arctic hares have white fur in the winter to hide on the white snow. In the short summer, they shed their white fur and grow brown fur instead.

Do you think the arctic hare's white fur coat is thick or thin?

Where does a striped skunk live?

Striped skunks live in a forest biome with many large trees. Some forests are hot and rainy, while others are cold. The leaves in the forest where these skunks live change color and fall off the trees when the weather turns cold and the days get shorter.

Striped skunks use their claws to dig burrows under the ground for sleeping during hot summer or cold winter days. Like the fennec fox, skunks are nocturnal and find their food at night.

While the skunk's white stripe warns other animals about its stinky spray, what color on the skunk would help it hide when it is active at night?

Where does a humpback whale live?

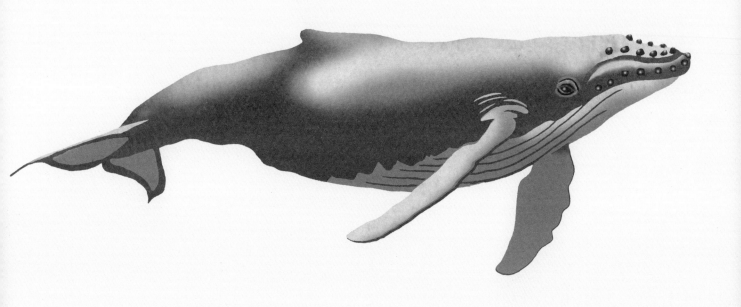

Humpback whales live in the water, which is the largest biome. This biome can be salty, like oceans, or fresh, like lakes and rivers. There are special kinds of plants and animals that live in the water.

Humpback whales are not fish, but are mammals, like the other animals in this book. However, instead of having hair or fur covering their bodies, they have a thick layer of fat under their skin to keep them warm. A whale can swim for long distances in the ocean using its tail and flippers.

Do you think it is easier to swim with hands or with flippers?

Do you remember which animal lives in which biome? Let's find out! Match the animal on the left with its biome home on the right.

VOCABULARY

Biomes: Places where plants
and animals that need the same kind
of rainfall and temperature live together.

Tundra: A windy, cold and icy biome where only a
few plants can survive.

Grassland: A fairly dry biome that has tall grasses
and very few bushes or trees.

Forest: A biome covered with large, tall trees.

Desert: A biome so dry that very few plants can grow.

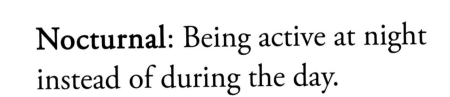

Nocturnal: Being active at night instead of during the day.

Arctic: The cold, icy land near the North Pole.

Burrow: A hole or tunnel under the ground where animals can live or hide.

Mammal: A group of mostly furry or hairy animals, whose mothers give birth to live babies and nurse them with their own milk.

Water (also called an *aquatic* biome): A biome covered in water.

For additional information on the animals found in
these biomes, as well as free teaching materials,
visit the Budding Biologist website at:

www.buddingbiologist.com